P9-CCB-089

THE JUDICIARY

LAWS WE LIVE BY

Lila Summer and Samuel G. Woods

A Blackbirch Graphics Book

RAINTREE
STECK-VAUGHN
PUBLISHERS

Austin, Texas

A Blackbirch Graphics Book

Printed in Mexico.

1 2 3 4 5 6 7 8 9 0 RRD 97 96 95 94 93 92

Library of Congress Cataloging-in-Publication Data

Summer, Lila E.
The judiciary: laws we live by / written by Lila Summer and Samuel G. Woods
p. cm.— (Good citizenship library)
Includes bibliographical references (p.) and index.
Summary: Discusses the law, the court system, how the law can be challenged, and what our laws mean to the individual.
ISBN 0-8114-7350-3 ISBN 0-8114-5578-5 (softcover)
1. Law—United States—Juvenile literature. 2. Courts—United States—Juvenile literature. [1. Law. 2. Courts.] I. Woods, Samuel G. II. Title. III. Series.
KF387.S86 1993
349.73—dc20 92-14199
[347.3] CIP
AC

Acknowledgments and Photo Credits

Cover: ©Blackbirch Graphics, Inc.; p. 4: National Archives; p. 7: ©Cynthia Johnson/Gamma-Liaison; p. 8: ©Bob Daemmrich/The Image Works; pp. 12, 15, 23, 26, 27, 28, 35, 38: AP/Wide World Photos; p. 13: ©Taylor-Fabricius/Gamma-Liaison; p. 14: ©Riha/Gamma-Liaison; p. 16: ©Frank Fisher/Gamma-Liaison; p. 20: North Wind Picture Archives; p. 22: Library of Congress Collection; p. 24: North Wind Picture Archieves; p. 29 (top): ©John Duricka/AP/Wide World Photos; p. 29 (bottom): ©Doug Mills/AP/Wide World Photos; p. 30: New York Convention & Visitors Bureau; p. 40: ©Jean Marc Giboux/Gamma-Liaison; p. 43: ©Stuart Rabinowitz.

Cover photo: Statue at the entrance to the U.S. Supreme Court represents the executor of law, holding the tablet of laws in his left hand.

Contents

We the People

insure domestic Tranquility, provide for the common

and our Posterity, do ordain and establish this Consti

Article. I

Section. 1. All legislative Powers herein granted shall be vested in a Congress of the United States, which shall consist of a S of Representatives.

Section. 2. The House of Representatives shall be composed of Members chosen every second Year by the People of the several S in each State shall have the Qualifications requisite for Electors of the most numerous Branch of the State Legislature.

No Person shall be a Representative who shall not have attained to the Age of twenty five Years, and been seven Years a Citiz and who shall not, when elected, be an Inhabitant of that State in which he shall be chosen.

Representatives and direct Taxes shall be apportioned among the several States which may be included within this Union, accordi Numbers, which shall be determined by adding to the whole Number of free Persons, including those bound to Service for a Term of Years, not taxed, three fifths of all other Persons. The actual Enumeration shall be made within three Years after the first Meeting of the Con and within every subsequent Term of ten Years, in such Manner as they shall by Law direct. The Number of Representatives shall thirty Thousand, but each State shall have at Least one Representative; and until such enumeration shall be made, the State of New entitled to chuse three, Massachusetts eight, Rhode Island and Providence Plantations one, Connecticut five, New York six, New J eight, Delaware one, Maryland six, Virginia ten, North Carolina five, South Carolina five, and Georgia three.

When vacancies happen in the Representation from any State, the Executive Authority thereof shall issue Writs of Election to f

The House of Representatives shall chuse their Speaker and other Officers; and shall have the sole Power of Impeachment.

Section. 3. The Senate of the United States shall be composed of two Senators from each State, chosen by the Legislature thereof Senator shall have one Vote.

Immediately after they shall be assembled in Consequence of the first Election, they shall be divided as equally as may be i of the Senators of the first Class shall be vacated at the Expiration of the second Year, of the second Class at the Expiration of the four Class at the Expiration of the sixth Year, so that one third may be chosen every second Year; and if Vacancies happen by Resignation Recess of the Legislature of any State, the Executive thereof may make temporary Appointments until the next Meeting of the Legislat such Vacancies.

No Person shall be a Senator who shall not have attained to the Age of thirty Years, and been nine Years a Citizen of the Un not, when elected, be an Inhabitant of that State for which he shall be chosen.

The Vice President of the United States shall be President of the Senate, but shall have no Vote, unless they be equally divided.

The Senate shall chuse their other Officers, and also a President pro tempore, in the Absence of the Vice President, or when he President of the United States.

The Senate shall have the sole Power to try all Impeachments. When sitting for that Purpose, they shall be on Oath or Af of the United States is tried, the Chief Justice shall preside: And no Person shall be convicted without the Concurrence of two thirds of the M

Judgment in Cases of Impeachment shall not extend further than to removal from Office, and disqualification to hold a Trust or Profit under the United States: but the Party convicted shall nevertheless be liable and subject to Indictment, Trial, Ju according to Law.

Section. 4. The Times, Places and Manner of holding Elections for Senators and Representatives, shall be prescribed in e thereof; but the Congress may at any time by Law make or alter such Regulation, except as to the Places of chusing Senators.

The Congress shall assemble at least once in every Year, and such Meeting shall be on the first Monday in Decem appoint a different Day.

Section. 5. Each House shall be the Judge of the Elections, Returns and Qualifications of its own Members, and a Majori … Business; but a smaller Number may adjourn from day to day, and may be authorized to compel the Attend … each House may provide.

… Members for disorderly Behaviour, and with the Co

CHAPTER 1

Democracy Hard at Work

Laws are the rules we live by every day. No one could get along well if we did not have laws. Laws keep us from doing just as we please without caring about the rights of others. Traffic laws are a good example. Walkers wait at stoplights because it is the law. School buses travel within the speed limit created by law. These laws maintain safety and at the same time they guard the rights of others.

An important part of law is that it can be enforced. Police officers see that our laws are obeyed. Courts are another way to enforce laws. The job of a judge in court is to make sure that we carry out our laws in a fair, or just, way. How we carry out our laws may sometimes be more important than are the laws themselves.

Opposite: The Constitution is the foundation of our legal system.

Judges and courts in our country carry out our laws in a regular way through our judiciary system. *Judiciary* comes from the Latin word that means "judge." A system is an organized way of doing things. A family is a kind of system. It has rules and regular ways of punishing members who disobey the rules. Our judiciary system is like a huge family with a set of rules. For the huge family of the United States, these rules are the United States Constitution. This document was created in 1789 when our new country began to form a permanent government. The Constitution lists the principles by which we should govern ourselves. It protects us as a group. It also protects us as individuals.

For example, burning our country's flag is not against the law. An individual has the right to burn our country's sign of freedom. At times, people who felt strongly enough to protest against something our government has done burned the flag to express their feelings. Some people believe individuals should not have this right. They say that our flag is a sign of our national unity, and no one should have the right to destroy it. President George Bush wanted to change our Constitution to say that flag burning is against the law. He advised Congress, our national lawmakers, to add this to our Constitution. However, Congress eventually decided that the individual's right to practice free speech in this way was more important. It decided that the individual's right to burn the flag did not harm our nation.

One of the things federal (national) courts are set up to do is test our laws. Judges in these courts can look over laws to see if they are fair to both individuals and our nation as a whole. For example, let's take another look at our national symbol, the American flag. Many states used to have laws about saluting the flag. In these states, every child in school was required by law to salute the flag and say the Pledge of Allegiance. At the same time, the Constitution states that everyone has the right to free speech and freedom of religion. That means that all citizens, no matter how old they are, are free to say and believe what they please, as long as they do not say or do anything that harms others. You may wonder what a state law about saluting the flag has to do with what the Constitution says about our freedom to practice religion and free speech. The following story will answer that question.

Citizens demonstrate in front of the Supreme Court building in Washington, D.C. Freedom of speech is one of America's most cherished freedoms.

A Challenge to a Law

The story begins one day in Massachusetts in 1935. A third grader refused to say the Pledge of Allegiance and salute the flag. Every child saluted the flag except Carelton Nicolls, Jr. Carelton was a Jehovah's Witness. This religious group thinks that saluting or pledging loyalty to a flag is worshiping it. And like many other religions, theirs forbids worshiping anyone or anything but God. Carelton was in trouble. Massachusetts law required students to salute the flag. Carelton was sent home from

Pledging allegiance to the flag is one way Americans can show loyalty to their country.

school. The next day, his father came with him to school. The father also refused to salute, and he was arrested for disturbing the peace. This made the Jehovah's Witnesses angry. One of their leaders made a speech about it on the radio. "Jehovah's Witnesses conscientiously object and refuse to salute the flag and pledge allegiance to it," he said.

Two young people in Pennsylvania heard this speech. They were fifth and seventh graders, William and Lillian Gobitis. They were Jehovah's Witnesses, too. They decided to stand up for what they believed. At school the next day, Lillian told her teacher, "I shall not salute the flag anymore." Lillian's classmates teased her and threw rocks at her. The school expelled her and her brother.

The children's father decided to go to court. He and other Jehovah's Witnesses asked a federal judge to decide who was right. They argued their case in a federal court in 1938. They wanted the right not to salute or say the pledge. The school insisted that the children should obey the law to honor our country. The judge (Federal District Judge Albert B. Maris) agreed with the Jehovah's Witnesses. This judge said that William and Lillian did have the right to refuse to salute. The Constitution protected their freedom of religion. The school could not force the children to salute the flag if doing so was against their religion.

An Appeal

That is not the end of the story. The school did not like this court's decision. The school had the right to ask another court to hear both sides again. They decided to go to a more powerful court, the Federal Court of Appeals. The judges in the Appeals Court did listen again to both sides, but they also agreed with the Jehovah's Witnesses. They said that William and Lillian did not have to salute and could go back to school.

The school still did not accept this decision. It appealed the case once more. This time, the school appealed to the highest court in the land, the U.S. Supreme Court. This court is called "supreme" because it has the last word, or final decision, in any U.S. case. The children's family felt sure that the Supreme Court would favor their side. After all, the lower courts had protected their constitutional right to practice their religion freely. Two courts had already agreed that the children did not have to salute. But they were surprised. In June 1940, the Supreme Court ruled in favor of the school. Of the nine judges, called "justices," of the Supreme Court, eight decided against the Jehovah's Witnesses. They reversed the decision of the lower courts. (Some people called these eight justices "conservative" because they decided not to change a law made by a state.) Chief Justice Felix Frankfurter said the children should obey the state. The state law could force children to salute the flag, he said.

One Against Eight

Only one justice disagreed. Justice Harland Fiske Stone did not think the Supreme Court should let states make laws that took away freedom of religion. He said the Constitution was supposed to guard the rights of minorities (people who don't follow what most others follow). Jehovah's Witnesses were the minority because most other religious groups did not think saluting the flag was wrong. But the rest of the justices outvoted him.

First Lady Eleanor Roosevelt spoke out in favor of the Jehovah's Witnesses. Finally, three of the Supreme Court justices changed their minds about the issue. "If we go back to court," the Jehovah's Witnesses thought, "we might win this time." So they took another case to court.

Their new case was much like the other one. In West Virginia, a school had expelled some young Jehovah's Witnesses for refusing to salute.

A Victory at Last

After a series of trials, the West Virginia school board appealed to the Supreme Court. The Court made its decision on national Flag Day, June 14, 1943. The Constitution, Justice Robert Jackson said, guards the individual's right to speak his own mind. Yet, he said, it does not force anyone to do or say what is not in his mind. Forcing Jehovah's Witnesses to pledge or salute violates their rights to free speech and religion. No one should be forced to agree or act with the majority, he said. At last, the Jehovah's Witnesses had won for good.

From all this we see that our judiciary system does not just enforce our laws. It also guards our rights under the Constitution. Sometimes a law and the Constitution do not agree. Then the judiciary system can help undo laws. Our Constitution lists the principles by which we should govern ourselves. But it does not tell *exactly* how. It is like a map. Judges and courts help us find our way as our country grows and our ideas change.

New Ideas Make New Laws

Laws are made to meet our needs. When these needs change, old laws can be undone and new laws may be written. New ideas and new inventions can call for new laws. For example, there were no traffic laws in our country before the invention of cars. New laws had to be written, too, as the telephone, television, videotape, and computer came into our

Suffragists fought to gain the vote for women in the early 1900s. Here, women march through the streets of New York in support of the Nineteenth Amendment.

lives. If you have rented a video to watch at home, you know that most videos include a note reminding you of the law against making a copy of the video. A law like this protects the people who make videos, so that they will not lose money because of people who have copied or stolen their work.

New ideas can help change our laws, too. Even our Constitution can change as our ideas do. For example, women were once not allowed to vote in our country. Only people who owned property (such as land or a house) could vote, and most women did not own property. A few women began to demand the right to vote. After a long struggle, women won the right to vote in 1920. Our government added this right to the Constitution through what is called an "amendment."

Two Important Issues

In the next few years, you may see many important changes in our laws and our Constitution. As ideas change, people challenge the laws we live under. In the news, you see protests over laws about abortion. Abortion is the procedure by which a woman ends her pregnancy if she does not want to have a baby. Some groups say that abortion takes away the rights of the unborn. These groups protest laws that allow abortion. Today, our courts listen to many cases about abortion laws. Some of these cases end up in the Supreme Court. It is likely that the abortion issue will remain a subject of debate for many years.

Laws about the death penalty are also challenged in our courts. Some states require that people who commit serious crimes, like murder, be put to death. People who argue against the death penalty feel that it is just as wrong to execute (kill) a murderer as it was for the murderer to kill in the first place.

Those in favor of the death penalty say that it protects our community from dangerous wrong-doers. These people also feel that many criminals are unable to ever rejoin society in a productive way.

Capital punishment—also known as the death penalty—has been the center of a national debate for many years.

Of course, not all arguments about laws are about life and death. For most of us, laws about our rights to privacy are closer to home. In school, you may feel that you have the right to keep things in your locker without anyone else's opening your locker. Some schools, however, allow teachers to search lockers. They believe a teacher should be able to check lockers for things that may be against the law, such as drugs. If a student broke the law by owning drugs, searching his or her locker would be one way to protect others from harm. On the other hand, our Constitution protects an individual's right to privacy. But does this right mean that a student can refuse to allow a teacher to open a locker? How can we protect our community and, at the same time, protect individual rights? Our judicial system helps us find answers to questions like these.

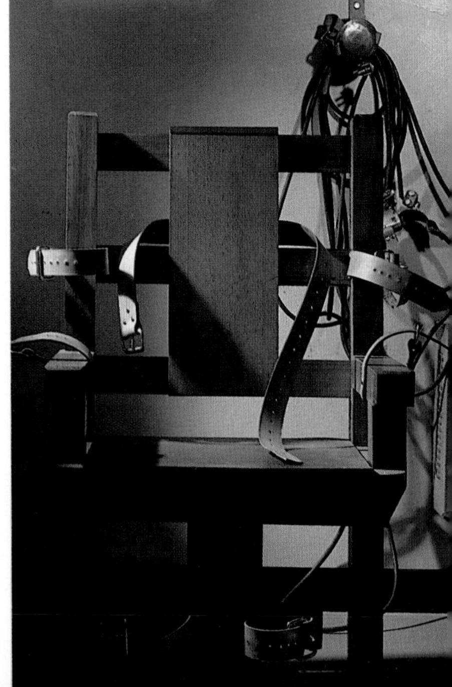

The first ten amendments to the Constitution—known as the Bill of Rights—were developed especially to protect the rights of individuals. Many of these amendments guarantee that certain rights cannot be violated, even if a person is arrested and charged with a crime. Police must follow strict rules in order to search or seize the property of a suspected criminal. They must also follow strict guidelines in arresting suspects and taking confessions. Many police and law enforcement officials complain that all these rules and regulations get in their way. They say that following all these lengthy procedures makes them less effective in fighting crime.

Before the 1960s, the police were not as carefully supervised as they are today. While investigating crimes or questioning suspects, police officers often broke the law themselves in order to get what they were after. It was common practice for police to break into a suspect's house and to take evidence. This evidence would then be used in court against the accused. Police often used force to get confessions from suspects. In the police station, prisoners would be punched or deprived of sleep in order to make them confess. These confessions were then used against the accused in court. By 1961, many people began to say that these police actions were violating the rights of individuals. They said that police officers needed to be more restrained.

A number of cases about police procedures were brought to the Supreme Court in the 1960s. In one case, *Mapp* v. *Ohio* (1961) [*v* stands for "versus" or "against"], the Supreme Court ruled that no court could use evidence that was obtained illegally. To legally search a property, police would have to first get special permission (called a warrant) from a judge. In order to issue a warrant, a judge has to be convinced that there is evidence on the premises. The Court also said that using force or other cruel actions to obtain a confession would make the evidence unusable in court.

Another famous case came in 1966. *Miranda* v. *Arizona* established the right of an arrested suspect to remain silent and consult a lawyer before making any statements to the police. Ernesto A. Miranda, who worked in a warehouse in Phoenix, Arizona, was arrested for rape and kidnapping. He confessed his crimes to the police but was never told that he could remain silent until his lawyer was present at any questioning. The Supreme Court decided that all arrests in the future must be made with an official declaration of the right to remain silent and to consult a lawyer. Today, if a prisoner is not read the "Miranda rights" at the time of arrest, any confession made is worthless in a court of law.

Ernesto Miranda was charged with rape and kidnapping in 1966. His case established some important guidelines for the treatment of people who are accused of serious crimes. *Left:* An arrest is made in Los Angeles.

CHAPTER 2

Community Justice

When people live in groups, rules must be obeyed. Thousands of years ago, people knew that wrongdoers must be punished. Murder, of course, was wrongdoing. When anyone killed another, the group lost an important member—a parent, a hunter, or a warrior. The group had to kill the murderer to protect the rest of the group. Sometimes the family of the murderer got even, or took revenge, by hurting those who had killed the murderer. Then others took revenge on the family in the same way. Sometimes murders like these went on for years.

It is easy to see that taking revenge is not a fair way to protect a group. As groups formed tribes,

Opposite:
Our judicial system requires the punishment of people who do not obey the laws of our society.

their chiefs came to have the power to punish wrongdoers. Members of the tribe saw that a chief could be the authority to keep order. The chief could have the last word about what was fair to protect the entire group. Chiefs, and later kings, became powerful judges and lawmakers.

Decisions by the King

In England, as in other countries, the kings held their own courts of law. Kings did not decide only about crimes like murder or stealing. They also settled arguments about everyday things. For example, if one farmer argued for the right to graze his sheep in his neighbor's wheat field, the king decided whether to let him. Often the king demanded some kind of payment for settling the case. He might decide to take some of the sheep or some of the farmland in return for making a decision.

The king could also determine punishments for certain crimes. For example, more than a thousand years ago, King Ethelbert in England (560–616) began a regular system of punishment. For the crime of cutting off another man's arm, the punishment was a fine: the wrongdoer had to pay a certain amount of money. For cutting off an ear, the wrongdoer had to pay a smaller amount. This system of punishment was an improvement over the older community justice of taking revenge.

Each king had a slightly different way of deciding punishments. As time passed, the kings' ways of settling cases became customs, or the common ways in which things were done. The king—or the officers he appointed—could decide how to settle a case by looking at how a similar case had been decided earlier. Today, courts also decide questions of law by looking at how similar cases were decided. These cases are called "precedents," and they help make up what we call "common law." Common law means law based on customs, or how things have been done in the past. In England, common law developed slowly over time.

When King Henry II of England began to introduce a new method of settling cases in the royal courts, people were eager to have their cases tried there. This new method was the trial by jury. Twelve men of the neighborhood would be summoned to help the judge (who was a royal official, not the local lord) decide the case. Unlike the members of a modern jury, the members of the old English jury were expected to know about the matters in dispute. In fact, they were both witnesses and jury.

Decisions by the Church

England's major church (the Protestant church) also became a powerful lawmaker. The church owned almost as much land as the king. Bishops (church leaders) began to hold their own courts. Villagers who worked on church land came to the bishops to settle arguments. Some of the ways in which

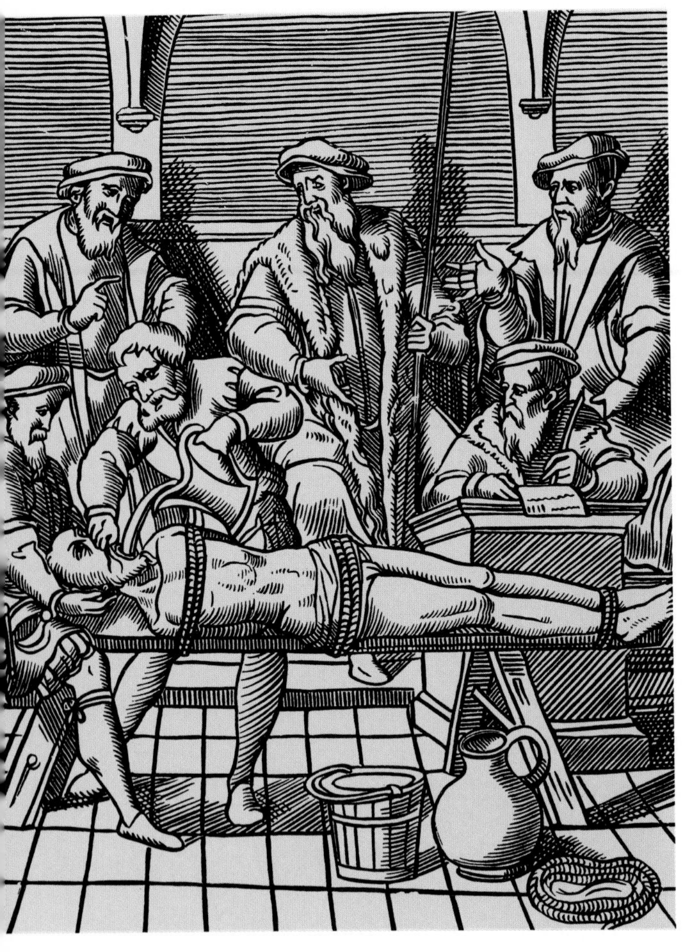

they decided innocence or guilt seem strange to us today. For example, someone accused of being a witch might be tied up and thrown into water. If the accused person floated, she or he was guilty. If the accused sank, he or she was innocent. The church thought that God would show the truth in this way.

Some church courts required "trial by ordeal." In this trial, an accused person might be forced to walk through burning hot coals. If the person made it all the way, he or she was declared innocent.

Before the 1200s, many people were subjected to cruel treatment in order to prove guilt or innocence. Here, a water torture is given to a suspected witch.

New ideas swept away many of these crude ways of deciding justice. During the reign of King John in England, the barons grew angry at the unjust ways in which their cases were decided in the king's court. King John could take their castles, plow up their meadows, or imprison their children if they did not do what he wanted. They decided to fight against these injustices. In 1215, the barons drew up a document known today as the Magna Carta. In it, they demanded the right to be judged only by other barons like themselves—their equals, or peers. (The word *peers* has two meanings: in the Magna Carta the reference just meant "equals"; but it is also sometimes used to mean "a member of the nobility." What makes things even more confusing is the fact that for a long time it was mostly peers, or nobles, who were entitled to be tried by their peers, or equals.)

Decisions by the People

When the English colonists came to the New World, they brought English law with them. They also brought their memories of how a judge can be unfair. As each colony formed its government, all 13 colonies made sure that the courts included juries of ordinary people. The colonists knew that ordinary people like themselves could help guard against an unfair judge.

The colonists fought the American Revolution to be free from a king's rule. Each colony became used to governing itself. Each had its own courts. It was hard for them to work together as a new nation. Yet they needed to unite under a central government. Leaders from the colonies gathered in Philadelphia in 1787 to write the principles of the new nation. They wanted a strong united government, but they did not want to take away the power of the individual states. They agreed to divide power between the federal (national) government and the state governments. The new Constitution

Americans fought the Revolutionary War to be free of England's king. As an independent nation, the colonists organized their own government in which the people ruled.

created federal courts to hear cases the states could not settle on their own. These are disputes (disagreements) between people from different states, those between the government of one state and that of another, and those involving treaties (agreements) with other nations.

The Constitution states that "the judicial Power of the United States, shall be vested in one supreme Court, and in such inferior Courts as the Congress may from time to time ordain and establish." This part of the Constitution, Article III, is the original plan for our highest, or most powerful, court. Later, Congress passed laws to create a larger judiciary system in more detail.

Nine Justices

When it was first written, our Constitution was a kind of experiment. It listed rules or principles to guide us in governing ourselves. At the time, no one was sure that the Constitution could really work. It called for a Supreme Court that would be the most powerful court in the land. Yet no one knew exactly what this high court should do. How could the Supreme Court help the Constitution work? How much power should this court have?

Those who served as judges on the Supreme Court helped answer these questions. John Jay was our nation's first chief justice, from 1789 to 1795. As the first chief justice, Jay established many of the early rules that governed the workings of the Supreme Court. One of the most important justices was Chief Justice John Marshall, who led the Supreme Court from 1801 to 1835. He was appointed by President John Adams, and led the Supreme Court when Jefferson, Madison, Monroe, John Quincy Adams, and Jackson were president. At the time, our nation was still poor after years of fighting the Revolutionary War. The state governments had not established good ways for working together. Other countries saw that we were not united enough to do business with them very well. Our country was like a family that was not sure how to work together for the good of everyone.

Chief Justice Marshall realized that a strong Supreme Court would help the country. Marshall

Chief Justice John Marshall was responsible for defining the power of the Supreme Court from 1801 to 1835.

wanted the Supreme Court to be independent. He did not want the president or Congress to be more powerful than the Court. To be independent, you must have some say about the rules you live by. Marshall thought the Court should be able to say when laws were constitutional. He fought for the power of the Court to look over laws to see if they fit in with the principles of the Constitution. "Judicial review," the power of the Court to look over a law in this way, is how the Court decides if a law is constitutional. Today, Congress can pass a law that it believes is constitutional. If the law is challenged, the Court makes the final decision about it.

In 1857, a slave named Dred Scott became the focus of a famous legal case about the rights and the freedoms of slaves.

The Dred Scott Case

Sometimes a strong Supreme Court has not been good for the country. During the days when slavery was practiced, Chief Justice Roger Taney made an unfortunate decision in his judicial review of an important case. In 1857, an enslaved man named Dred Scott traveled with his owner and lived in a state where slavery did not exist. A claim was made that, because of this, Scott was or could be a free man. Here was the chance for the Court to decide on laws about enslaving others. The Supreme Court decided that an enslaved person was the property of the owner and remained a slave as long as the owner wished. The decision meant that Congress could not pass any laws to limit slaveowners' rights and that slaves had no rights.

Congress had previously divided new territories into some that were slave states and others that were free states. Now this decision meant that what Congress had done was unconstitutional. The final decision of the Supreme Court was to allow slavery. The country agreed that the Court was the final authority on this constitutional question. Today, everyone agrees that the decision in the Dred Scott case was a mistake. It helped bring on the Civil War. That war won freedom from slavery for African Americans.

Changing the Constitution

From the very beginning, there were ways to change the Constitution. Such a change is called an amendment. When the Constitution was first proposed, many people refused to vote for it unless the government promised to add some amendments. The first 10 amendments are called the Bill of Rights, and they include important rights that guarantee freedom of speech, press, and religion; rules that say the government cannot search a person's house without getting permission from a judge; and rules guaranteeing a fair and open trial.

After the Civil War, Congress added some more amendments. They were written especially to protect the rights of people who had once been enslaved. One of these, the Fourteenth Amendment, says that everyone has the right to "the equal protection of the laws." But some states still made laws to try to keep people of color from voting, owning property, and having other common rights. For example, many state laws forced white and African American children to go to separate schools.

Brown v. *Board of Education*

Nearly 100 years after Justice Taney's term, another important Chief Justice, Earl Warren, made a famous decision. An African American girl in Kansas, Linda Brown, wanted to go to a school that was, by Kansas law, all white. Linda's family did not think she could get an equally good education at her school. Her father challenged the law that required her to go to an all-black school.

In this court case, called *Brown* v. *Board of Education of Topeka* (1954), the Court decided in favor of integrated (racially mixed) schools. Chief Justice Warren said that school segregation [separation] by state law causes a feeling of inferiority in black children that seriously hurts them. He then concluded that public-school segregation by state law violates the equal protection clause of the Fourteenth Amendment. Consequently, the laws that separated, or segregated, races in the schools were declared unconstitutional. Today, children of all races go to school together because of this decision. Many people believe that this case was the beginning of true civil rights in our country.

The lawyer who argued for the Browns in this case was named Thurgood Marshall. He is some-

Thurgood Marshall was the first African American to serve on the Supreme Court. His career was marked by many important cases involving civil rights.

Dr. Martin Luther King, Jr. (center), led the fight for civil rights in the 1960s. His wife, Coretta (also shown), was also a driving force in the civil rights movement.

times called Mr. Civil Rights. He worked for the National Association for the Advancement of Colored People (NAACP), a group that fights for racial equality. Many people think that his help in winning Linda Brown's case paved the way for the Civil Rights Act of 1964, which enforced school desegregation. The next year, Congress passed the Voting Rights Act, which helped guard the rights of African Americans to vote in local and national elections. These new laws allowed African Americans to use the courts to fight for justice. Marshall became a Supreme Court justice, the first African American to do so, in 1967.

Selecting a Supreme Court Justice

The nine justices of the Supreme Court decide questions that are important to all of us. They serve "on the bench" for their lifetime. Who these men

Sandra Day O'Connor was the first woman to serve on the Supreme Court. O'Connor was appointed in 1981 by Ronald Reagan.

and women are matters to all of us. The president "nominates," or names, someone to be a justice. Then a special group of senators, the Senate Judiciary Committee, examines that person's abilities and past experience. The committee then tells Congress its opinion. Finally, Congress votes to approve or reject the candidate.

Since the Senate committee meetings, called "hearings," are on television today, anyone can watch how a Supreme Court justice is approved. Some law experts and others complain that this public process is like a political campaign. They believe picking a new justice for the Supreme Court should not be done in public. Others believe that we the public have a democratic right to be part of this important selection.

In 1988, President Reagan nominated Judge Robert Bork to serve on the Supreme Court. Because of his conservative views, Bork's nomination turned into a national debate that was televised across the nation for weeks. Bork became so unpopular that Congress did not approve his nomination. In 1991, President Bush started another national debate when he nominated Judge Clarence Thomas to replace Thurgood Marshall. As happened with Bork, Clarence Thomas's views became the subject of a national debate that concerned millions of people. Despite the great controversies surrounding Thomas, he was eventually approved by Congress.

★★★★★★ THE THOMAS–HILL "TRIAL" ★★★★★★

Television viewers could make up their own minds as they watched Clarence Thomas answer the questions of the Senate Judiciary Committee. Just before the hearings were over, something happened that had never happened before. On television, before millions, a candidate for Supreme Court justice was accused of wrongdoing. A woman accused Thomas of sexual harassment, which means unfairly bothering a person of the opposite sex. The woman, Anita Hill, was a lawyer who had worked for Thomas in Washington, D.C., several years before. The committee asked her to tell them her side of what happened. The hearings became a kind of trial without a court.

Hill said that Thomas harassed her by making indecent jokes about dating her and about various sexual activities. Thomas replied that he had never done anything like that.

Some viewers felt that checking into Thomas's private life on international television was not fair. Without being accused of a crime and without having a judge or jury, he was on trial in front of millions. They worried that his good name or reputation would be unfairly hurt. Thomas said to the senators, "I think I've died a thousand deaths." He meant that he suffered because of unfair accusations. He added that he was "losing belief in the system," that the process of broadcasting the hearings made a spectacle of him and the way justices are approved. But others said that the televised hearing was fair. The morals or ethics of a justice should be beyond doubt, they said. No one is sure if either side is right. What is certain is that television has brought the approval process of a Supreme Court justice into everyone's home.

STATE AND FEDERAL COURT SYSTEMS

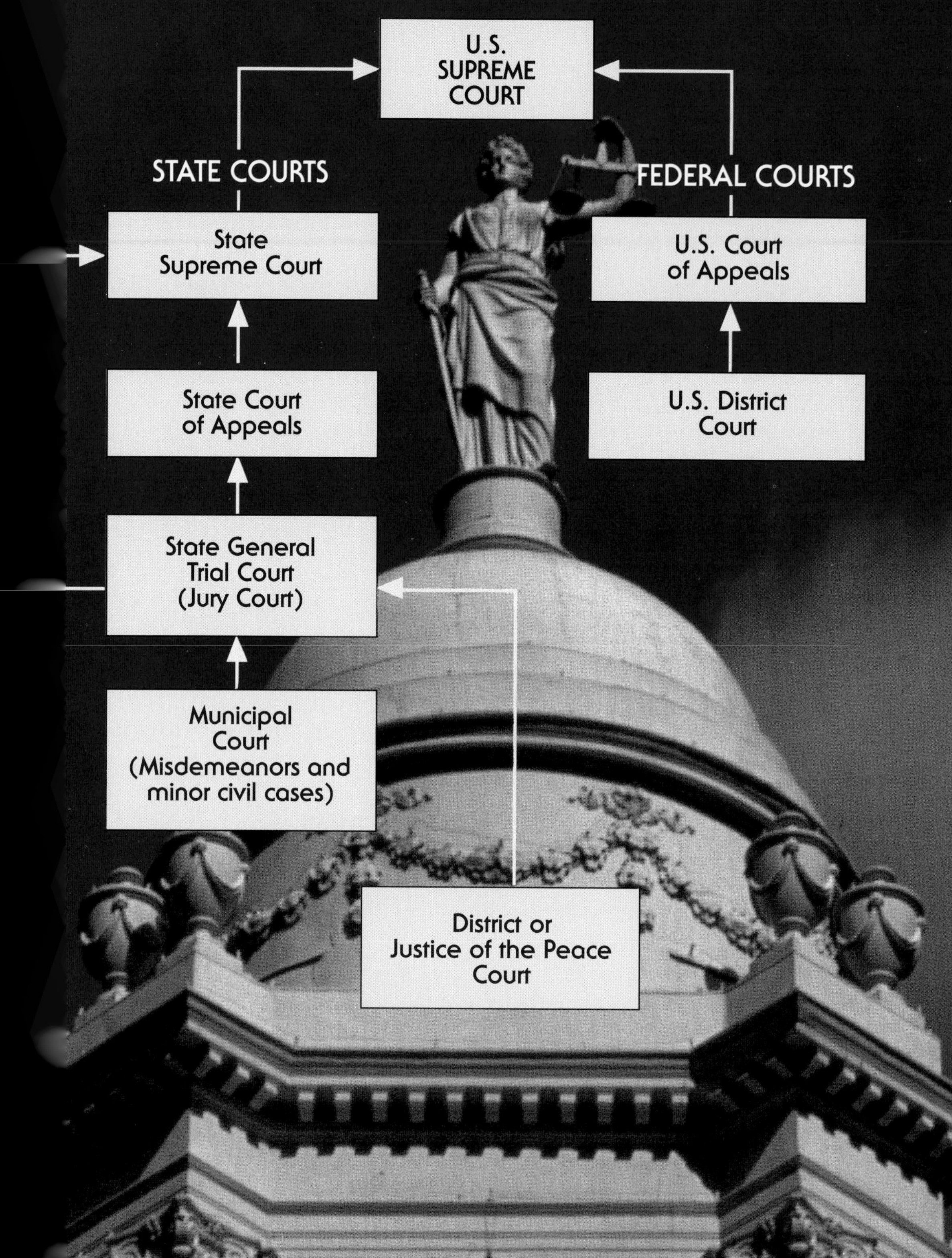

C H A P T E R 3

Our Court System

Courts in the United States are responsible for three major functions. First, they must make sure that the laws of the land are followed by everyone. To do that, they must interpret the laws that are made by the lawmakers in the state and federal governments. Second, courts must punish those who are found guilty of breaking laws. And third, the courts must also be sure to protect the rights of all individuals. As the courts review laws, they must consider how to use a law so it is fair to the people of our country.

In order to best protect the rights of individuals, the judicial system works differently from other branches of government. Its officials are appointed

Opposite:
A case may reach the United States Supreme Court through either lower federal (U.S.) courts or state supreme courts.

rather than elected. And their jobs are usually guaranteed for a long time. In some cases, such as the Supreme Court, a justice is appointed for a lifetime. This means that judges and justices are in many ways "above politics." Because they do not have to worry about public opinion polls and getting reelected, they are free to make decisions based only on what they believe is right. The framers of the Constitution felt that this system would insure fairness and justice for all people.

The Kinds of Courts

There are many different kinds of courts in the American judicial system. But any court in America will fall into one of two categories. Either it will be a federal court or it will be a state court. Each court is designed to decide certain kinds of cases.

The Federal Courts

Some cases involve interpreting (explaining) the U.S. Constitution. These cases are decided in federal courts. Matters of constitutional rights can come up in any kind of case. Often, federal court cases are between an individual and a state or federal government. Sometimes federal cases are between two individuals. Whoever is involved, a federal case demands that the Constitution be consulted for an answer. But the Constitution is written in a way that is open to much interpretation. Many lawyers, juries, and judges have different understandings of exactly what the Constitution's words mean. The opinion of one judge will not necessarily be the opinion of another judge who hears the exact same facts of a case presented.

The Process of Appeal

The American court system is designed to deal with the differences in legal opinions. If either of the parties involved in a case believes the case was not settled fairly, they can "appeal" to a higher court. That means a court with greater authority must listen to the case and give its opinion. Certain cases can be appealed all the way to the Supreme Court. If the Supreme Court decides to hear the case, its decision will be final. If it declines an appeal, the ruling of the court beneath it stands as the final word on the matter.

U.S. District Courts. In the federal court system, the lowest courts are the U.S. district courts. These courts are the basic trial courts of the federal system. There are approximately 90 federal districts scattered throughout the United States and its territories. Each district has a district court. For each of these courts, there is a district attorney. A district attorney represents the federal government in the cases that are tried in federal district courts.

U.S. Courts of Appeals. There is a theory behind the basic structure of the federal court system. That theory says that a trial in one court and an appeal to another is usually enough to provide justice. The next step up from district courts is the court of appeals. The appeals court exists to make sure every party that wants an appeal can have one.

There are 11 courts of appeals in the United States. The country is divided into 10 regions, or "circuits," plus the District of Columbia. Each circuit has a court of appeals. The number of judges assigned to each court varies, but at least two judges must hear each case presented.

If a case from a U.S. court of appeals is further appealed, there is only one place for it to go: the U.S. Supreme Court.

The Supreme Court. Located in Washington, D.C., the Supreme Court is the most powerful court in the nation. Its decisions are final. There is no court higher to which one can appeal.

The Supreme Court is made up of eight justices and one chief justice. Like judges on all federal courts, the justices are appointed by the president of the United States, with the advice and approval of the Senate. Supreme Court justices are appointed for a lifetime and may be removed only by a complicated process called "impeachment."

The Supreme Court is most powerful because it can review the decisions of any court below it. If it decides to hear a case, the Supreme Court's decision is the final word. It can reverse decisions that other courts have taken months or years to reach.

Getting a case heard by the Supreme Court is not easy. Before the Court will hear a case, it must

be recommended by the Court's official reviewers. Once a case is recommended, the justices decide whether they will hear the case. Most cases never make it to that point. Because so many cases are presented to the Court for review, the justices must pick the cases they will hear very carefully. And the cases must raise key (important) constitutional questions of great concern to our nation.

The new Supreme Court in 1992: *(From left)* Clarence Thomas, David Souter, Antonin Scalia, Sandra Day O'Connor, Chief Justice William H. Rehnquist, John Paul Stevens, Harry Blackmun, Byron White, and Anthony Kennedy.

The State Courts

The state court system handles most of the legal business of our nation. Though the Supreme Court decisions get the most publicity, they are only a small part of all the decisions given by courts each year. Most cases are tried in state courts. And most legal decisions are given by state courts.

The state court system has almost the same structure as the federal system. The only difference is that there are more state courts in the chain. Like the federal system, the states have lower courts, higher courts, courts of appeals, and state supreme courts.

Minor Courts. At the bottom of the state court system are the minor courts. These are courts that deal with the simpler issues of day-to-day government, such as domestic problems, traffic violations, and other common matters.

State General Trial Courts. The general trial courts are the courts that conduct most of the business of the nation. Individual states divide their areas into different judicial regions. Some states assign courts by county, others assign courts by a district that may have one or more counties in it. Still other states may have a circuit that is made up of many districts.

The trial courts are responsible for hearing cases involving more serious matters. These include criminal cases, settlements of estates, and guardianship problems for children or property. In most states, those accused of crimes are entitled to a trial by jury. This means a trial that has 12 citizens in a petit jury, or 12 to 23 citizens in a grand jury, "peers" of the accused, who listen to the facts. These "jurors" then offer a decision to the judge, who has also listened to the case. In most instances, the judge will accept the jury's decision. In some cases, the judge can "throw the jury's verdict out" if he or she feels there weren't enough facts for a fair decision to be made.

State Court of Appeals. A case that was tried in a general trial court can be appealed to a higher court. Sometimes the case will go to the state appeals court. There, judges examine the cases that are brought before them from the trial courts. Often the judges will decide if the original verdict was fair or not. Their judgments in many types of cases are final. But when questions about the state or federal constitution are raised, the case may be appealed once again. This time, the case will go to the state supreme court.

State Supreme Court. The state supreme court is the highest court in the state. Like the U.S. Supreme Court, the state supreme court has several justices and a chief justice. This court is the final authority on questions of law within the state. Its interpretation of state laws and the state constitution cannot be overruled, even by the Supreme Court (unless a state law specifically goes against the U.S. Constitution).

If the state supreme court hears a case that raises questions about the U.S. Constitution, then the case may be appealed to the highest court in the nation for a final decision. As we have already learned, the Supreme Court reviews cases from state supreme courts and U.S. courts of appeals to decide which cases it will eventually hear.

Criminal suits are brought by a state or federal government against people accused of serious crimes.

The Two Kinds of Cases

You have already learned that different courts consider different kinds of cases. These cases are usually further divided into one of two categories: criminal cases or civil cases.

Criminal Cases

Criminal suits are cases brought by the state or federal government against a person or group of persons. In a criminal case, the government is accusing someone of having broken a law. These cases usually involve serious crimes such as murder, rape, assault, drug trafficking, kidnapping, and theft. The goal in a criminal case is to obtain justice by punishing the person or people who have broken the law. Often, punishment comes in the form of a prison sentence or a fine, or both.

Civil Cases

Civil suits are cases brought by one person (or persons) against another person (or persons). These persons are known as "parties." In a civil lawsuit, a "plaintiff" sues a "defendant" for causing damage to a person or property. In some cases, the plaintiff may claim that the defendant directly caused the damage (by setting a fire, for example). In other cases, the plaintiff may try to prove that damage was indirectly caused by the defendant (for example, a person slips on an icy walkway outside a store and sues the storekeeper). In all of these civil cases, the plaintiff is seeking money to make up for the damage that was done by the defendant. Damage can be in the form of emotional hardship or trauma, as well as in the form of physical injury to a person or a piece of property.

Sometimes civil suits can involve criminal actions. For example, if a person is run down by a drunken driver, the victim may sue for damages in a civil suit. It is also possible that the state will file criminal charges of drunken driving against the same driver. In this case, the civil and criminal trials would be held separately.

STOP

CHAPTER 4

What Our Laws Mean to You

Until your 18th birthday, the United States considers you too young to be independent. For that reason, many of our laws are designed to protect young adults from harm and from making bad decisions.

If you are under the age of 18, you are legally called a "minor." A minor is someone who has not yet been given all the legal privileges of an adult. Legally, a minor cannot vote, join the military, or buy or drink alcohol. Until age 16, it's illegal for a minor to stay out of school. All of these restrictions have been designed to protect young adults from making decisions that can have harmful results. Many young adults feel that these laws are unfair. They feel that they are old enough at age 14 or 16

Opposite: **In our judicial system, minors are treated differently from adults.**

to make their own decisions. But the government must declare an age at which you are legally considered an adult. That age, for now, is 18.

You don't have to wait until you are 18 to do *everything* grown up. In most states, a person can learn to drive and get a driver's license by the age of 16 or 17. A 16-year-old can also get working papers and hold a steady job.

Legal Issues About Age

Our judicial system makes another distinction between minors and adults. It says that certain actions taken with a minor are a crime, even though similar actions with another adult are not crimes. The distinctions are mostly made in areas concerned with sex. For example, if an adult has sexual relations with a minor, it is legally defined as "statutory rape." The government says it is a crime for an adult to have sex with anyone under 18 years old. Even if the minor agrees, it is still considered a crime.

Laws about statutory rape were made to protect minors from sexual abuse and from entering into relationships that they are not mature enough to handle. Having sexual relations requires a great deal of responsibility. It means carefully considering all the consequences. And it means being able to deal with any outcomes that may arise. Just as is the case with drinking, smoking, or joining the military, the government feels minors are not old enough to make wise decisions about these matters.

Minors are also protected against all the various kinds of child abuse, including neglect. While you are a minor, you must have a legal guardian. A legal guardian is an adult who is responsible for your well-being. In most cases, parents are the legal guardians of their children. As guardians, these people have a legal obligation to take care of their minors. They are responsible for feeding and clothing their minors, and for keeping their minors away from dangerous or threatening situations. If an adult or guardian fails to provide basic and responsible care for a minor, that adult can be charged with the crime of child abuse.

Sexual abuse by a guardian (or any adult) is also a serious crime. Sexual abuse includes incest and rape. These actions are crimes against minors not old enough to defend or care for themselves.

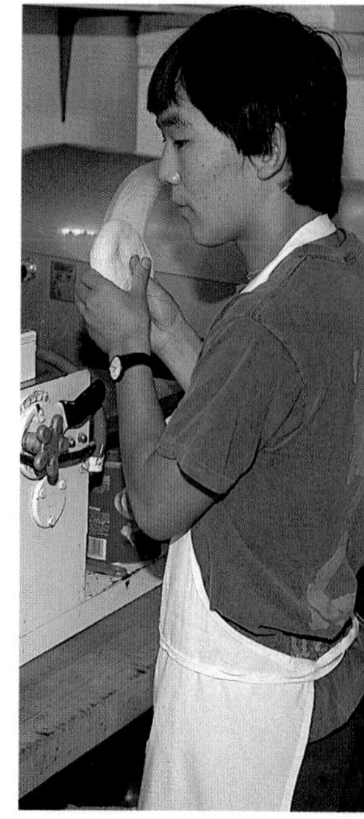

In most states, minors can get working papers and hold steady jobs by the time they turn 16.

The Juvenile Justice System

In our country, legal procedures for minors are different from those for adults. That is because the government believes that young people who break the law do not always need to be treated as harshly as adults. A 14-year-old who commits a robbery, for example, will not go directly to jail. An adult who committed the same crime, however, would probably serve a sentence.

There is a separate legal system in America that deals with minors who break the law. This system is called the juvenile justice system.

How Does the Juvenile Justice System Work?

There are two ways that a minor can be involved in the juvenile justice system. The first is to be taken into custody for breaking a law. This means that a police officer or court officer takes the minor to a juvenile detention center. A juvenile detention center is like a jail for young adults.

The other way a minor can become involved in the juvenile justice system is by being a constant source of trouble or danger. Minors who are constantly out of control and whose parents are unable to supervise them are often called PINS. This word stands for "Person In Need of Supervision." PINS are often absent from school, have run away from home, or have constant fights with their parents. PINS can be brought to a juvenile detention center even if they have not broken a specific law.

Due Process

Minors, like adults, are entitled to "due process" under the law. Due process means that all of an individual's rights must be respected. It means that specific steps must be taken at each stage of the legal process. Many of the principles of due process were set down in the Constitution's Bill of Rights.

At some point, a judge will hear a minor's case. At that time, the judge can do one of three things. First, a judge may order "probation." This means that, under the careful supervision of a probation officer, the minor can be released back into society.

The second action a judge can take against a minor is to order enrollment in a reform school. This is a very strict school that is run like a prison. Minors in reform schools take classes and learn to be productive members of society.

The third action a judge can take against a minor is reserved only for very serious crimes. In these cases, a judge may order that the minor be tried as an adult. This means that the case would be sent to a regular judge in the criminal court system.

Recently, drugs have caused the number of serious and violent crimes to rise. At the same time, the average age of violent criminals has dropped. Rising statistics for murder, armed robbery, rape, and drug trafficking have caused more and more minors to be tried as adults. If a judge tries a minor as a juvenile, the sentence cannot last beyond the minor's 21st birthday. If the minor is tried as an adult, the sentence can go on for much longer.

An Overview

Although our laws change over the years, the founding principles of our judicial system have not changed in over 200 years. Those principles guarantee that everyone in our nation will be protected equally under the law. And they guarantee the right to a fair trial, with fair punishment for a crime. Most important, those principles guarantee every American the right to exercise the many freedoms that make our country so special.

Glossary

amendment A change to the Constitution.
appeal Transferring a case to a higher court for rehearing.
capital punishment The death penalty for committing serious crimes.
civil rights The rights of all citizens to vote and to equal treatment under the law.
common law Law based on how things have been done in the past.
debate To discuss reasons for and against something.
defendant The party that is sued by a plaintiff in a lawsuit.
ethics The standards of conduct and moral judgment.
hearing An appearance before an investigative committee.
impeachment The charging of a public official with wrongdoing.
judiciary The part of the government that administers justice.
laws Rules of conduct established by the authority of a nation.
minorities Racial, religious, or political groups that differ from the larger, controlling groups.
nominate To name someone for consideration to a certain position.
peers People of the same rank or ability; equals.
plaintiff A party that sues a defendant in a lawsuit.
precedents Earlier cases that serve as examples for similar new cases.
right The power or privilege belonging to one by law.
segregation The policy of separating racial groups.
suffrage The right to vote.
verdict The formal finding of a judge or jury.

For Further Reading

Green, C. and Sanford, W. *The Judiciary.* Vero Beach, Florida: Rourke Publishing, 1989.
Greene, Carol. *Sandra Day O'Connor.* Chicago: Childrens Press, 1982.
Jenkins, G. *The Constitution.* Vero Beach: Rourke Publishing, 1989.
Robins, Dave. *Just Punishment.* New York: Franklin Watts, 1990.
Sgroy, Peter. *The Living Constitution.* Westwood, New Jersey: Silver Burdett Press, 1987.

Index